God's Little Faces
from
Many Different Places

By: Mary Feather Thomas

Trilogy Christian Publishers
A Wholly Owned Subsidary of Trinity Broadcasting Network
2442 Michelle Drive
Tustin, CA 92780

For information, address Trilogy Christian Publishing
Rights Department, 2442 Michelle Drive, Tustin, Ca 92780.
Trilogy Christian Publishing/ TBN and colophon are trademarks of Trinity Broadcasting Network.

For information about special discounts for bulk purchases, please contact Trilogy Christian Publishing.

Manufactured in the United States of America

10 9 8 7 6 5 4 3 2 1

Library of Congress Cataloging-in-Publication Data is available.

ISBN 979-8-88738-506-8 (Print Book)
ISBN 979-8-88738-507-5 (ebook)

This book is dedicated to my beautiful grandchildren, Olivia Ruth, Violet Elizabeth, Louisa Mary Jean, Andrew Benjamin, and "Baby Springtime" who will grace us with his angelic presence in the spring of 2023. Since this book may be published before he is born, I refer to him as "Baby Springtime." My grandchildren ignite my world with incredible joy and gratefulness. They are truly the light of my life on this earth. May they always embrace God's beauty in all human beings. This book is also dedicated to the grandchildren of my siblings: Julio, Felipe, Manuel, Blanca, Pedro, Virginia, Olga, Georgia, Elle, and John.

I want to acknowledge my granddaughters, Olivia, Violet, and Louisa, for contributing to the ideas for the illustrations of this book. Lastly, the inspiration for this book would never be possible without the power of example of my parents, Gregory and Grace. They taught me to embrace the beauty in all human beings. I know they are dancing in heaven right now.

God makes all these little faces
from many different places.
Love, His special ingredient!

1

He makes faces from the West to the East,

From the United States to the Caribbean Islands.

3

To the Orient.

God makes little faces from
many different places.

6

Different faces live across the street.

8

Some different faces live across the seas.

9

Some faces have blue eyes,
brown eyes, hazel eyes or green!
God sees beauty in them all,
for all the world to see.

11

You see, God made us in His image, so faces can
be black, white, yellow, red, or brown.
But one thing is certain, God smiles when He sees all the
different faces of His children and never, ever, frowns.
Yes, God loves His little faces from many different places.

...ts them all to become ...nds and play.

You see, God does not have favorites. To Him, they are all precious works of art.

15

God makes many different faces from many different places.
They include you and me.

God's little faces are a rainbow
for all the world to see.

17